Embracing Change:

Overcoming Obstacles of Career Transitions

TREVA BENDY

3G Publishing, Inc.
Loganville, Ga 30052
www.3gpublishinginc.com
Phone: 1-888-442-9637

First published by 3G Publishing, Inc. September, 2024.

ISBN: 9781941247709

Printed in the United States of America

Library of Congress Copyright: TXu002440106/2024-07-18

Embracing Change:
Overcoming Obstacles of Career Transitions

Table of Contents

Embracing Change:
Overcoming Obstacles of Career Transitions

Welcome!

Welcome to *"Embracing Change: Overcoming Challenges of Career Transitions."* If you're feeling a mix of excitement and nervousness about changing careers, you're in good company. This book is designed to support, educate, and empower anyone ready to navigate the uncertainties of a career change. Inside, you'll find a wealth of practical advice, psychological insights, thought-provoking questions, and actionable steps tailored to help you move from your current position to a role that aligns more closely with your career aspirations.

No matter where you are in your career—whether you're a seasoned executive, an entry-level employee, or somewhere in between—this book is tailored for you, especially if you're feeling unfulfilled or noticing downturns in your industry. Like many others, you may face common challenges such as fear of the unknown, financial concerns, a sense of lost identity, and lack of support. This book is designed to address these issues, providing you with the strategies needed to navigate both personal desires for growth and external changes in the job market. **At the back of the book,** you'll find the ***Take Action Now!*** section, designed to help you reflect on and align with your career and personal goals. This section **compiles the thought-provoking questions** from **throughout the book,** providing space for you to think through and **write your answers as you encounter each question**. With these insights and tools, you'll be empowered to take confident steps toward a more fulfilling and successful career.

Embracing Change:
Overcoming Obstacles of Career Transitions

About Treva Bendy

My story began in the heart of New Orleans, Louisiana, a city full of life and culture. My childhood was a journey, moving from one city to another until we finally established our home in the diverse city of Houston, Texas. Growing up, education was always emphasized as the key to success, but I often wondered what true success really meant. With my aunt's guidance and encouragement, I pursued a degree in Industrial Engineering, which wasn't easy. It was very challenging, and at times I was afraid I might not graduate, but I didn't let those fears stop me. Instead, they motivated me to work even harder to succeed. And I did! Upon graduating, my initial goal was to secure a position in Industrial Engineering, but I soon found myself drawn to the field of Instructional Design, which appeared more intriguing and aligned with my interests. This shift into Instructional Design was fueled by a deepening fascination with the processes of learning and development, along with a desire to channel my engineering skills into a creative and educational realm. My background in Industrial Engineering sharpened my skills in project management, analytics, collaboration, and problem-solving, which laid a solid foundation for my career transition into Instructional Design. **Despite the initial uncertainties**, this career change presented a valuable opportunity for both personal and professional growth. It steered me toward a field that not only resonated more profoundly with my interests but also provided immense satisfaction and fulfillment. With over 20 years of enriching experience as an eLearning and career transitions coach specializing in Instructional Design, working with top-tier global organizations in the energy and technology sectors, I have not only glimpsed but grasped the essence of success. To me, success is about overcoming obstacles, continuously learning, and using that knowledge to help others through education.

Chapter 1: Understanding Career Transition

Introduction

When you wake up for work in the morning,

do you feel invigorated and ready to take on

new challenges, or do you find yourself

counting the minutes until the day ends?

<u>Note</u>: *As you encounter each question in this book, Take action now by reflecting on and writing your response in the **Take Action Now!** section before moving on.*

This question isn't just rhetorical—it's a critical starting point for understanding when it might be time to consider a career change. In today's rapidly evolving job market, staying attuned to personal satisfaction and professional growth is not just beneficial; it's essential. This chapter is designed to clearly explain what a career transition entails and why it's crucial for your growth. It will offer a detailed guide to help you recognize when and why a career change might be necessary. By distinguishing between a routine job change and a substantial career transition, you'll gain the insights needed to strategically plan and execute these changes. This will enable you to align your career moves with your personal and professional development goals, ensuring that each step you take is both purposeful and impactful.

What is Career Transitioning?

Career transitioning involves various changes people make to align their professional lives with their personal goals, seize new opportunities, or enhance their quality of life. These changes may include moving to a different industry and learning a new skill, transitioning to different roles within the same field, starting a business, or adjusting work schedules to better accommodate personal needs, such as spending more time with family. Some transitions are abrupt and significant, like relocating to a new city or moving from a traditional full-time job to freelancing to gain greater flexibility in work hours. Others may occur more gradually, such as slowly accepting more responsibilities in a current role or reducing work hours to ease into retirement.

Career transitions are often sparked by a mix of internal and external factors that motivate individuals to seek new opportunities. On a personal level, someone might seek a new career that brings more happiness, provides growth opportunities, or better aligns with their core values and personal beliefs. These internal triggers push people to think about what they really want from their careers and make changes to achieve that. On the other hand, external triggers like changes in the industry, new technologies, changes in the job market, or economic downturns can also drive career transitions. These factors might force someone to adapt to new conditions, move to an industry that's growing, or update their skills to stay relevant. Together, these personal motivations and external pressures often lead to the decision to change careers.

How could understanding the specific type
of career transition you are undergoing
change how you prepare for your future?

Key Statistics and Trends

Recent trends show the integration of AI and automation in the workplace is transforming job roles. While this technology is enhancing productivity and creating new job opportunities, it also requires workers to develop new skills to stay competitive. Soft skills like creativity, emotional intelligence, and problem-solving are becoming increasingly important as technical tasks are automated (BusinessBecause). Therefore, automation is changing the types of jobs available, especially in areas like technology, renewable energy, and healthcare. Looking to the future, work trends suggest a move towards more remote work opportunities, short-term contracts, and freelance jobs, which offer more flexibility. Industries expected to grow include artificial intelligence (AI), cybersecurity, and biotechnology, while traditional areas like manufacturing might shrink due to the impact of automation and changes in consumer needs. This evolving landscape requires professionals to continuously update their skills and stay flexible to succeed in a competitive market.

Chapter 2: The Catalysts of Change

Introduction

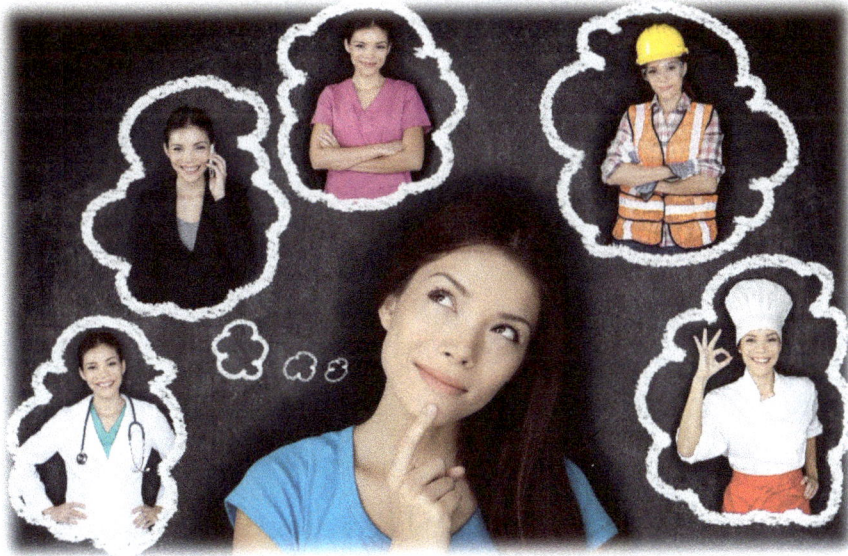

As jobs change with technology and the economy, are you excited to explore new career opportunities, or do you feel pressured to rethink your current path?

The professional landscape is continually being transformed by economic factors, technological advancements, and social trends. These external forces shape job availability and create new career opportunities. For instance, the rapid growth in digital technology has led to the creation of entirely new job categories in fields like data science, digital marketing, and cybersecurity—areas that were almost unheard of just a decade ago.

Embracing Change:
Overcoming Obstacles of Career Transitions

In this chapter, we'll explore both the internal motivations and external pressures that trigger individuals to rethink their career paths. We'll look at personal drivers like the desire for greater job satisfaction and personal growth, alongside external influences such as technological shifts, economic changes, and evolving industry demands. Additionally, we will offer insights on how to recognize the right time for a career change, providing practical examples and advice to help you navigate these transitions smoothly and progress toward more fulfilling opportunities.

External Catalysts

Technological advancements are changing many industries and the types of jobs available, requiring people to learn new skills and consider different career paths. Innovations like artificial intelligence (AI), automation, and remote work platforms are leading these changes. AI and automation are making some jobs obsolete, especially those involving repetitive tasks, and are creating a need for skills that machines can't replicate. At the same time, the growth of remote work has changed not just where we work, but how we work, requiring more digital skills and the ability to self-manage effectively. These changes are opening new opportunities in technology-driven fields and requiring workers in all areas to adapt to work environments where digital skills are more critical. This shift highlights the importance of continuous learning and being flexible with your career plans.

Economic shifts and globalization have a strong impact on job markets and career choices. For example, the global financial crisis of 2008 and the more recent economic challenges caused by the COVID-19 pandemic led to job losses in many sectors, pushing people to look for work in more stable industries. On the other hand, economic booms, especially in technology with the rise of e-commerce and digital services, have created many new jobs that require advanced skills.

Globalization has significantly expanded job opportunities by integrating global markets. As companies venture into new countries, they not only create jobs in these emerging markets but also require workers to be adaptable, culturally savvy, and able to navigate diverse business practices. These changes illustrate how major economic shifts and global trends can push people to change careers or modify their approach to existing roles to stay competitive in the job market.

Regulatory changes can deeply affect various industries by creating new requirements that demand different skills or roles. For example, in healthcare, new rules about patient privacy and telemedicine have increased the need for experts who understand these regulations, as well as IT professionals skilled in managing digital health records and online medical services. In the finance sector, laws introduced after the 2008 financial crisis have increased the demand for compliance officers and risk management experts to help institutions meet new, stricter standards. In education, updates on how schools must be accredited, and the growth of online learning have led to a greater need for teachers who can effectively use digital platforms and develop online courses. These examples show how changes in laws and regulations can require professionals in affected fields to learn new skills or shift to new roles to keep up with industry demands.

Internal Catalysts

Career plateaus often occur when individuals feel they've reached a 'ceiling' in their current jobs, where further growth or advancement seems unlikely. This can lead to a sense of stagnation and dissatisfaction, motivating them to look for new challenges or growth opportunities. When facing a plateau, people might look for ways to move up or change roles within their current organizations or even consider switching to entirely different industries where they can apply their skills in new ways. This period often pushes individuals to improve their skills or get additional education to become more attractive to potential employers. Ultimately, hitting a career plateau can be a strong incentive for professionals to rethink their career goals and seek positions that offer better prospects for personal and professional growth, helping them stay relevant in a rapidly changing job market.

Personal life changes frequently prompt individuals to reevaluate their career paths. Significant events like relocating for a spouse's job, becoming a parent, or caring for an elderly family member can dramatically shift your priorities. These moments often bring about a deeper reflection on what is most important in your professional and personal life, leading to changes in career direction to better align with these new realities. Relocation often opens up opportunities in different geographic areas, while becoming a parent usually requires more flexible working hours or a job closer to home. Similarly, taking on caregiving responsibilities can make full-time employment difficult, urging individuals to consider part-time roles, freelance work, or entirely new careers that provide a better balance between work and personal life. These life changes often lead people to reshape their careers to better fit their new situations and needs.

Many individuals are motivated by the desire to find work that resonates with their personal values and makes a positive impact on society. This need for meaningful work can lead to significant career changes as individuals seek roles that meet their professional needs, match their ethical standards, and contribute to the greater good. For example, someone might switch from a corporate position to work at a non-profit that focuses on environmental protection or social justice, finding more fulfillment in making a positive difference. These career changes go beyond simple job satisfaction; they connect individuals with work that matches their values and has a meaningful impact on the world, leading to more fulfilling and purposeful job experiences.

Burnout and job dissatisfaction often result from ongoing stress and a lack of fulfillment at work. When stress builds up over time without relief, it can lead to burnout, leaving individuals feeling drained and unable to meet the demands of their job. This can make it very difficult for someone to continue in their current job effectively, pushing them toward considering a career change as a necessary step for their health and overall happiness. Making such a transition can offer a fresh start and a more satisfying work experience, helping to renew a person's energy and passion for their work.

"Choose a job you love, and you will never have to work a day in your life." –
Confucius

Recognizing the Need for Change

Recognizing the need for change in your career is an important step that can greatly influence your job satisfaction and growth. Self-assessment tools are practical resources, like quizzes and questionnaires, designed to help you figure out if you're ready for a career change and what your main reasons might be for considering one. These tools ask questions about your current job satisfaction, your interests, skills, and values. By answering these questions honestly, you can better understand whether a career change makes sense for you right now, and if so, what kind of changes you might be looking for. This can be an important step in ensuring that your career move is well thought out and aligns with your personal and professional goals.

Another key indicator of the need for change is persistent dissatisfaction or lack of advancement. If you find yourself constantly watching the clock or dreading each workday, it's a clear sign that something needs to give. Such feelings can wear down your well-being and hinder your professional growth, signaling that a new direction might be necessary. Paying close attention to feedback from colleagues, mentors, and neighbors is essential. Their perspectives can provide a fresh look at your work performance and satisfaction, helping you determine when it might be time to explore a different career path. This external feedback can highlight strengths and weaknesses that you may not see, offering clues about whether a change could benefit your professional growth and personal happiness. Finally, it's important to stay informed about trends in your industry. Monitoring changes in job demand, emerging skills, and the overall health of the industry can provide valuable indicators of when it might be necessary to adjust your career focus. By keeping up-to-date and continually reflecting on these trends, you can more effectively navigate your career path and make decisions that enhance your job satisfaction and professional fulfillment.

Are you listening to subtle cues from your professional life, or are you ignoring them?

Preparing for Change

Preparing for change involves more than just practical steps; it also requires getting ready emotionally. This part of the process means learning how to handle the fear of the unknown and building up your resilience. Resilience enables you to recover from setbacks and keep going even when things get tough. To harness this strength effectively, it's important to recognize and confront any anxieties or doubts you may have about changing careers. Techniques such as talking through your feelings with friends, a coach, or a counselor, practicing mindfulness, and setting small, manageable goals can all help you feel more secure and confident as you navigate through change. This emotional preparation ensures you are ready to take on new challenges and equipped to handle the stresses that come with them.

Updating your skills and knowledge is crucial when preparing for new career opportunities. This process, often called upskilling or reskilling, involves learning new skills or improving existing ones to match the requirements of the job market. Being proactive about learning not only makes you a more attractive candidate for future jobs but also keeps you competitive in your field. It's important to identify the skills in demand within your desired industry and find ways to acquire them, whether through online courses, certification programs, workshops, or self-study. This commitment to continuous learning helps ensure that you are always ready to take advantage of new opportunities as they arise.

Embracing Change:
Overcoming Obstacles of Career Transitions

Expanding your professional network is a powerful way to gain insights into different industries and discover potential job openings. By connecting with more people in your field or the fields you are interested in, you can learn about the current trends, the skills in demand, and the real challenges and opportunities in those areas. Networking can happen through social media platforms like LinkedIn, attending industry conferences, or joining professional groups. Talking to experienced professionals can provide you with a clearer picture of what different jobs entail and may even lead to direct job referrals. Essentially, the more people you know, the better your chances of finding new opportunities and gaining valuable information that can help steer your career in the right direction.

Chapter 3: The Emotional and Psychological Journey

Introduction

When considering a career change, do you

feel excited about new opportunities, or do

you find yourself uncertain about leaving

your familiar work environment?

When we think of career change, it's often the practical steps that come to mind: updating a resume, networking, or learning new skills. However, the emotional and psychological journey that accompanies this transition is equally critical and far less discussed. Changing careers isn't just a professional move; it also brings about a range of emotions and mental challenges. In this chapter, we will explore the common feelings people experience during this time, such as anxiety, excitement, uncertainty, and even fear of the unknown. We'll also discuss the psychological hurdles that can arise, like dealing with the loss of a familiar work environment or the stress of stepping into the unknown. Understanding and managing these emotional and psychological responses is key to navigating your career transition smoothly and successfully.

Understanding the Emotional Rollercoaster

Understanding the emotional rollercoaster of career transitions is crucial, as it helps individuals navigate the complex feelings associated with change. The process often begins with **Initial Shock and Denial**, where the impact of leaving a familiar job sets in. Recognizing this resistance to change is the first step, and managing it effectively involves seeking support and reassurance from friends or mentors who can guide you through this unsettling phase.

As you progress, you might experience **Frustration and Despair**, especially when faced with setbacks such as job rejections or difficulties in acquiring new skills. During these challenging times, it's important to stay resilient. Setting small, achievable goals can help maintain your motivation and gradually restore your confidence.

Following this, you'll enter a phase of **Gradual Acceptance**. Here, you start to recognize and embrace the possibilities that your new career path offers. It's a time for positive reflection, allowing yourself to get excited about the future and the opportunities that lie ahead.

The journey concludes with **Renewed Hope and Excitement**. This stage is marked by a significant increase in enthusiasm and energy as you begin to engage fully with your new career. With a clearer view of the potential benefits, you can channel your energies more effectively, ensuring a successful adaptation to your new role or industry. *Implementing mindfulness and stress-reducing techniques during these phases helps maintain emotional balance.* Techniques such as deep breathing, meditation, and regular physical activity can serve as anchors, stabilizing emotions much like steadying a ship in stormy waters.

Understanding Change

Could recognizing and embracing each phase of this emotional rollercoaster be the key to mastering your career transition?

Psychological Models of Career Transition

Transitioning careers isn't just about what you feel; it's also about understanding why you feel it. Models like the *Kubler-Ross Change Curve, Bridges' Transition Model,* and *Prochaska and DiClemente's Change Cycle* provide frameworks that help make sense of these emotional journeys. By applying these models, individuals can anticipate what comes next, preparing themselves mentally and emotionally for the road ahead.

The **Kübler-Ross Change Curve**, initially developed to describe the stages of grief, is also useful for understanding how people react to significant personal and professional changes. This model identifies five stages people typically go through when they experience significant change, such as a career transition. To effectively use the Kübler-Ross Change Curve in managing a career change, it's important to recognize and understand each stage as you encounter it. This allows you to apply specific strategies to handle the emotions and challenges that arise. Here's a guide on how you can navigate the five stages effectively:

1. **Denial:** Initially, there might be a refusal to believe the change is happening. For career transitions, this could manifest as ignoring the signs that it's time to move on from a current job or doubting the reality of a new job opportunity.

   - **Acknowledge Your Feelings:** Understand that it's normal to feel disbelief or denial about needing a career change. Acknowledge these feelings rather than ignore them.

- **Seek Information:** Start gathering information about the realities of your current job market and potential opportunities. Information can often mitigate the impact of denial by confronting it with facts.

2. **Anger:** As the reality of the situation sets in, frustration and anger can arise. This could be directed towards oneself, colleagues, or even the situation stemming from feelings of helplessness or unfairness.

   - **Express Your Emotions Safely:** Find healthy ways to express your frustrations, such as talking to a trusted friend, writing in a journal, or engaging in physical activity.

   - **Seek Support:** Discuss your feelings with a mentor or counselor who can offer professional advice and emotional support.

3. **Bargaining:** At this stage, individuals might attempt to negotiate a way to avoid or lessen the impact of the change. In the context of career transitions, this might involve trying to salvage aspects of an old job or making compromises on career goals.

   - **Evaluate Options Realistically:** Rather than clinging to what was, start to look at what could be. Consider all possible options, even those that might initially seem less appealing.

   - **Prepare for Compromise:** Understand that perfect scenarios are rare, and being open to compromise can lead to unexpected opportunities.

4. **Depression:** Realizing that change is inevitable can lead to a sense of loss and sadness.

- **Allow Yourself to Grieve:** It's important to let yourself feel sad about the losses associated with your career change. This might include the loss of colleagues whom you've built relationships with that provided emotional support and camaraderie, and their absence can lead to feelings of isolation; it might include the loss of a familiar routine that provided a sense of stability and predictability and lastly, it may include aspects of your identity in that your previous job likely contributed significantly to your sense of identity and self-worth. This often means redefining your identity, which can be challenging and may involve a period of introspection and self-discovery.

- **Professional Help:** If feelings of sadness are overwhelming or persistent, consider seeking help from a mental health professional.

5. **Acceptance:** Finally, individuals come to accept the change. This means embracing the new job or career path and beginning to look forward with optimism.

  - **Embrace the New:** Acceptance is a vital stage where you embrace the new opportunities. Start setting new goals and planning your path forward.

  - **Stay Positive and Active:** Engage actively with your new environment and continue to seek out activities and networks that can support your new career path.

The **Bridges' Transition Model** provides a clear framework to differentiate between "change" and "transition." Change refers to external events like losing or starting a job, while the transition is about the internal psychological process you experience as you adapt to these changes. To use this model effectively, you need to understand and work through its three phases: *Ending, Losing, and Letting Go; the Neutral Zone;* and *the New Beginning.* Here's a guide on how to navigate the three stages:

1. **Ending, Losing, and Letting Go:** The first phase involves dealing with the emotional impact of ending what was familiar. This might mean grieving the loss of old colleagues or the comfort of a routine you had mastered. It's important to acknowledge these feelings of loss and actively work through them.

   - **Acknowledge Your Losses:** Recognize and accept the emotions associated with the end of an era. Whether it's the loss of colleagues, a familiar work environment, or a previous role, acknowledging these feelings is crucial.

   - **Seek Support:** Talk about your feelings with trusted friends, family, or a counselor. Support groups can also be beneficial.

   - **Allow Time for Adjustment:** Understand that it's okay to feel unsettled and that these feelings are part of the process.

2. **The Neutral Zone:** This is the middle stage where the old situation is gone but the new hasn't fully begun. Here, you might feel uncertain and anxious about the future. It's a critical time for reflection and patience, where you are encouraged to slow down and explore what change means for you. This

period can also be a creative time, where you begin to get a clearer sense of your options and start planning your next steps.

- **Reflect and Reevaluate:** Use this time of uncertainty as an opportunity to reflect on what you truly want from your career. Think about your strengths, values, and passions.

- **Experiment and Explore:** Try out new roles, activities, or hobbies that align with your career interests. This exploration can provide insights into what you might want to pursue next.

- **Plan Ahead:** Begin to formulate a plan based on your reflections and any new insights you've gained. Setting short-term goals during this phase can help you move forward gradually.

3. **The New Beginning:** In this final phase, you start to accept and embrace the new changes. This means developing a new identity, discovering a new sense of purpose, and starting to move forward with renewed energy and commitment. Activities might include setting new career goals, taking on new roles, or implementing new skills.

- **Embrace the New Start:** Start to implement the changes you've planned. Engage with new opportunities and be open to learning from them.

- **Build New Relationships:** Establish connections with new colleagues and networks in your new role or industry. These relationships can provide support and open further opportunities.

- **Stay Positive and Resilient:** Maintain a positive outlook and be patient with yourself as you adapt to new circumstances. Celebrate small victories along the way to motivate yourself.

Prochaska and DiClemente's Change Cycle, also known as the **Stages of Change Model**, outlines a sequence of steps people typically go through when making any change, including career transitions. This model is especially useful for self-directed career changes as it focuses on the internal process of change. This is important when you are guiding your career in a new direction without outside triggers. Based on six steps, here's how you can use this model to effectively manage and guide your career transition:

1. **Precontemplation:** In this initial stage, you might not even be thinking about changing careers. You may be unaware of the need for change or in denial about your dissatisfaction with your current job.

   - **Awareness Building:** Begin by educating yourself about potential career opportunities and the benefits of change. This might involve researching career options, reading testimonials of others who have successfully changed careers, or discussing possibilities with mentors.

2. **Contemplation:** Here, you start to think about the possibility of change. You recognize that there are benefits to making a career shift, but you might also be aware of the potential drawbacks or risks. This is a stage of uncertainty where you weigh your options.

   - **Assessment and Reflection:** Take time to honestly assess your current job satisfaction and what you hope to achieve in a new career. Reflect on what is important to you in a job and what might be lacking in your current role.

3. **Preparation:** Once you decide that the benefits of changing careers outweigh the costs, you move into the preparation stage. This involves gathering information, possibly upgrading skills, or networking. You make practical plans and set a timeline for your career transition.

   - **Goal Setting and Planning:** Define clear, actionable goals for your career change. Start planning by identifying the steps you need to take, such as additional training or building a network in your new industry.

   - **Resource Gathering:** Collect resources that will support your transition, such as courses for skill development, resume-building services, or professional associations.

4. **Action:** This is where you actively begin to change your career. Actions could include applying for new jobs, starting further education, or launching a freelance career. It's a phase of significant personal effort and visible changes.

   - **Implementation:** Put your plans into action. This could include applying for jobs in your new field, attending networking events, or starting a new certification course. Actively seek out and create opportunities for advancement toward your new career.

   - **Feedback Integration:** Use feedback from your actions to refine your approach and improve your chances of success. Adjust your strategy as needed based on real-world experiences and outcomes.

5. **Maintenance:** After initiating the change, the maintenance stage involves continuing the actions that help sustain your new career path. This might include ongoing learning, further networking, or continual development of new skills to ensure long-term success in your new field.

   - **Sustaining Change:** Continue the behaviors and strategies that are working well in your new career. Keep learning and adapting to maintain your momentum and prevent regression.

   - **Support Systems:** Build and maintain support systems that can provide encouragement and advice as you settle into your new role.

6. **Termination:** This stage is unique, especially when applied to career changes. Unlike other life changes, career development is rarely static and often continues to evolve. However, in the context of this model, termination doesn't mean the end of your career growth but rather represents a stage where you've successfully settled into your new role or industry. At this point, you feel fully adapted and comfortable in your new environment, and the idea of reverting back to your previous career or old job habits no longer feels tempting or necessary. This stage signifies the successful completion of the transition cycle, where the new career path becomes a natural part of your professional identity and daily life.

   - **Reflection and Integration:** Once you feel that you have fully adapted to your new career—when the new behaviors have become second nature—it's important to reflect on the journey and integrate the lessons learned.

- **Future Planning:** Consider the next steps in your career development. Even after a successful transition, ongoing planning can help you continue to grow and advance.

By applying these models, you can strategically navigate your career transition, ensuring that you are not just reacting to changes but actively shaping your career path toward greater fulfillment. Each stage of these models offers insights and practical actions that can help you smoothly transition from one career to another, minimizing stress and maximizing success.

Strategies for Emotional and Psychological Resilience

Navigating a career transition successfully requires building emotional and psychological resilience. Begin this process by prioritizing self-care: maintaining physical health through regular exercise, a balanced diet, and adequate sleep directly impacts mental well-being. Engaging in relaxing hobbies and strengthening your social support network also provides significant emotional comfort and stability.

Integrating mindfulness and stress-reducing techniques into your daily routine can greatly assist in managing stress. Practicing mindfulness meditation, deep breathing exercises, or yoga helps you stay centered and reduce anxiety, enabling you to remain focused and present during times of uncertainty.

Embracing Change:
Overcoming Obstacles of Career Transitions

Developing a resilient mindset is essential for handling the emotional challenges of career change. Utilize techniques such as positive thinking, affirmations, and visualizing success to build mental fortitude and prepare for potential hurdles.

Family and friends form a foundational layer of emotional support, offering reassurance and encouragement when facing uncertainties or challenges. This personal network provides a stable base for venting frustrations, sharing successes, and receiving honest feedback - all crucial for making informed decisions.

Expanding your professional networks by joining peer support groups and professional associations can further reinforce your transition. These networks connect you with individuals who share similar professional interests and may have navigated similar transitions. They offer valuable networking opportunities, resources, and insights that are not readily accessible otherwise. Professional networks can also serve as a source for job leads, recommendations, and endorsements, accelerating your career development.

Mentorship plays a critical role in career transitions. Engaging with a mentor—an experienced professional in your field—can provide guidance, advice, and emotional support. Mentors offer insights gained from years in the industry, guide and advise you on career decisions, and help you overcome professional challenges. The support from a mentor can enhance your confidence, help refine your goals, and open doors to new opportunities.

Finally, recognize when professional help is needed. If stress becomes overwhelming, or if you need someone to discuss your career shift with, consulting a coach, counselor or therapist can be extremely beneficial. Utilize professionals who specialize in career transitions, career counseling, or stress management. Seeking professional help is a vital step in maintaining mental health during transitions.

By employing these strategies, you create a comprehensive approach to your career transition, ensuring a smoother process and successful adjustment to new roles and environments.

"Change your thoughts and you change your world." – Norman Vincent

---

Chapter 4: Cultivating the Right Mindset for Career Transition

Introduction

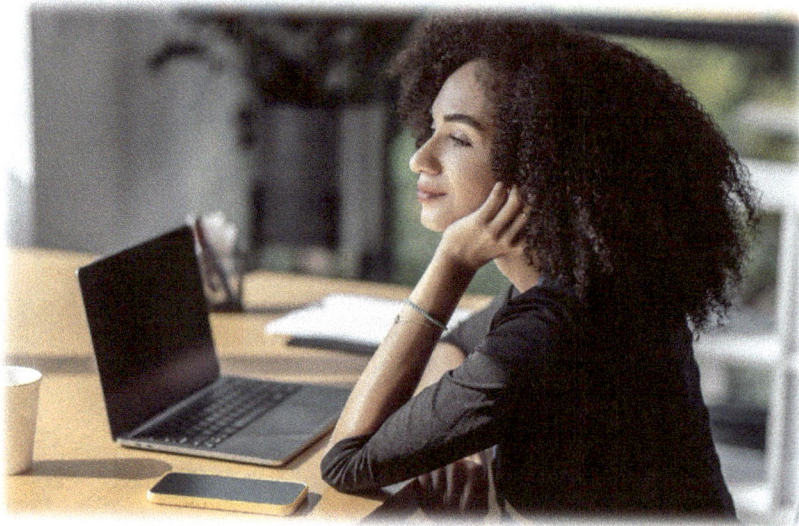

***During your career change, do you face
each day with a positive mindset, eager to
embrace new challenges, or do you struggle
to adapt and overcome obstacles?***

The journey through career change is as much about internal transformation as it is about external achievement. **Mindset plays a pivotal role** in this process, influencing how you perceive and respond to challenges. In this chapter, we'll explore how various mindsets can significantly impact your ability to adapt and succeed in new career paths. Adopting a proactive and positive mindset is essential—it's as important as having the right skills for a successful career transition. We'll discuss why adopting the right mindset is key to overcoming challenges and capitalizing on opportunities during your career transition. Additionally, you'll learn how to develop a mindset that builds resilience, encourages continual learning, and promotes positive change. This foundation is essential for navigating the complexities of career transitions effectively.

Growth vs. Fixed Mindset

Carol Dweck, a renowned psychologist and professor at Stanford University, is very influential and famous for her work on the psychology of mindsets, particularly the concepts of growth and fixed mindsets and their significant impact on career development. Carol's framework is based on her research into how people's beliefs about their own abilities affect their motivation and consequently their performance in various aspects of life, including education, work, and personal development.

Individuals with a **fixed mindset** believe that their abilities, intelligence, and talents are static traits that can't be changed. They think they have a set amount of intelligence, and there's little they can do to alter it. This belief drives them to want to appear smart at any cost, leading them to avoid challenges, give up quickly when faced with difficulties, ignore constructive feedback, and feel threatened by others' success. As a result, they often stop improving, reach a standstill in their development, and fail to achieve their full potential.

On the other hand, individuals with a **growth mindset** believe that they can develop their abilities and intelligence through dedication, hard work, and feedback from others. They embrace challenges, keep going when things get tough, learn from criticism, and are inspired by others' success. People with this mindset feel in control of their skills and understand they can improve through effort and continuous learning.

Carol Dweck's research shows that the mindset we adopt influences a great deal of our behavior and our interaction with others. For instance, in educational settings, students with a growth mindset are more likely to embrace learning more freely and exhibit a resilience that is essential for great accomplishment. Similarly, in the workplace, employees with growth mindsets are more likely to embrace challenges, learn from feedback, and achieve higher levels of success.

Dweck's framework doesn't just shed light on how we can succeed academically and professionally; it also offers actionable steps for developing a growth mindset. It stresses the importance of praise and feedback that focus on effort rather than natural talent, encouraging a mindset geared toward growth and continuous improvement. This approach has led to the widespread adoption of Dweck's methods in educational programs, corporate training, and personal development efforts, making her concepts essential for unlocking and nurturing human potential.

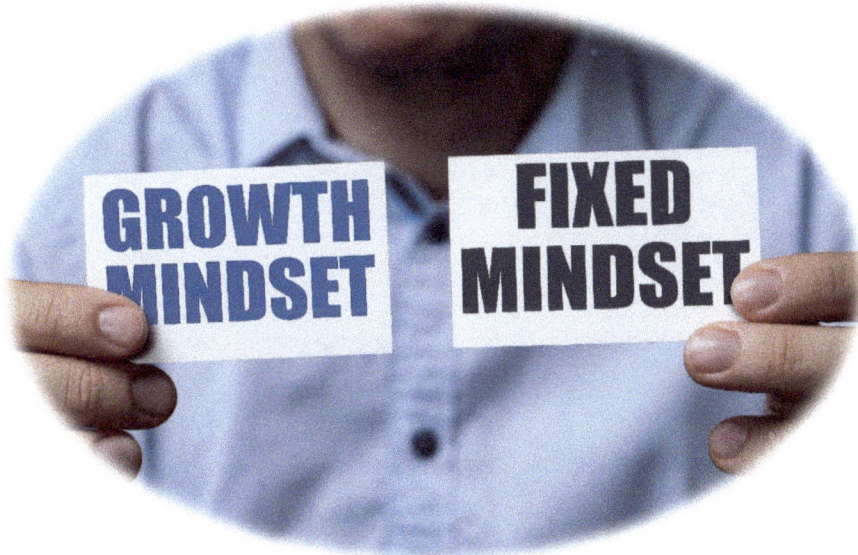

Could recognizing and fostering a growth
mindset be the key to unlocking your full
potential in your career transition?

Adaptability and Openness to Change

Adaptability in career transitions enables you to effectively adjust to new environments and meet changing expectations. Being adaptable allows you to quickly learn new systems, integrate into different teams, and conform to new corporate cultures, which are essential for smoothly transitioning into and succeeding in a new role.

Cultivate openness to new experiences by stepping out of your normal routine and trying new hobbies or volunteering in roles different from your usual job to gain new perspectives and skills. These activities enhance your flexibility and willingness to embrace change. Engaging in diverse experiences not only expands your worldview but also equips you to handle and adapt to the various adjustments that occur during career transitions more effectively.

To further enhance your adaptability, engaging in practical exercises such as scenario planning and role-playing can be incredibly beneficial. Scenario planning helps you anticipate various potential situations in your new role and develop strategies to manage them, preparing you for diverse outcomes. Role-playing, on the other hand, allows you to rehearse your responses to specific scenarios in a safe, controlled environment, which sharpens your reaction skills and improves your adaptability in real workplace situations. These exercises strengthen your psychological flexibility, better preparing you to navigate the complexities and dynamics of your new career path.

Was there a specific moment when you realized how important adaptation is in your career?

Confidence and Overcoming Imposter Syndrome

Building confidence through small, successive achievements is a powerful method for strengthening self-belief in your ability to succeed. This approach involves setting manageable goals and gradually tackling them one by one. Each success, no matter how minor it may seem, helps to reinforce belief in your abilities. As victories accumulate, confidence naturally grows, affirming the capability to achieve your objectives.

Alongside building confidence is combating imposter syndrome. Imposter syndrome is the feeling that you're not as competent as others perceive you to be, which can undermine your confidence and increase feelings of anxiety. To fight this, start by reframing negative thoughts. When you catch yourself doubting your abilities, challenge these thoughts with evidence of your past successes. Regularly remind yourself of your accomplishments, and actively tell yourself that you are skilled and deserving. It could be as simple as taking a moment to reflect on what you've achieved or sharing your successes with friends or colleagues. These practices not only help you overcome feelings of being an imposter but also contribute to a stronger, more resilient sense of self.

Curiosity and Continuous Learning

Curiosity and continuous learning are essential for maintaining adaptability and achieving long-term satisfaction in your professional life. Committing to lifelong learning helps you stay relevant and adaptable with the rapid changes in today's job market, which is crucial for both career advancement and personal fulfillment.

To foster a curious mindset, actively seek out new information and experiences relevant to your field. This could involve staying current with the latest industry trends by reading articles, reports, and news feeds. Participating in workshops and seminars not only broadens your knowledge and skills but also provides valuable networking opportunities. Moreover, reading extensively, both within and beyond your industry, can inspire new ideas and innovations that can significantly enhance your work and career prospects.

Developing a personal learning plan is an effective way to ensure your professional growth aligns with your career goals. Begin by clearly defining these goals and identifying the necessary skills and knowledge needed to achieve them. Include both formal education options, such as courses and certifications, and informal learning opportunities, like on-the-job training or online tutorials, in your plan. It's important to regularly review and adjust your learning plan to stay aligned with your evolving career objectives and the dynamic demands of the job market. By diligently following this plan, you ensure continuous growth and development, keeping your career path engaging and successful.

Embracing Failure as a Steppingstone

Embracing failure as a steppingstone is essential for career growth and building resilience. By shifting your perspective on failure—from viewing it as a setback to seeing it as a valuable learning opportunity—you can transform how you approach challenges. Recognizing that each failure offers a chance to learn and grow allows you to become stronger and more skilled. This mindset encourages you to take calculated risks and strive to innovate, which are key behaviors for advancing your career. With this approach, you're better equipped to tackle current challenges and seize future opportunities.

Developing effective coping strategies for handling setbacks is equally important. Stress management techniques such as mindfulness, exercise, and engaging in hobbies can help maintain your well-being and keep you focused. Additionally, having a supportive network of colleagues, mentors, and friends is invaluable. They provide encouragement and advice that help you navigate through tough times, offering different perspectives and insights that are essential in overcoming setbacks and moving forward. By reframing how you view failure—seeing it as a learning opportunity—and using these strategies to manage stress, you can transform challenges into catalysts for growth and success.

Emotional Intelligence

Enhancing your emotional intelligence through self-awareness, empathy, and effective communication is essential for understanding and managing your emotions, as well as improving your interactions with others. Here's how you can develop this skill:

1. Increasing your **self-awareness** is the first step. It involves recognizing your own emotions and understanding how they affect your thoughts and actions. You can cultivate self-awareness through activities like journaling, engaging in mindfulness practices, or obtaining feedback from peers. Being aware of your emotional triggers enables you to control your reactions and make decisions with greater clarity.

2. Developing **empathy** allows you to understand and share the feelings of others, which can deepen your connections. You can enhance your empathy by practicing active listening—paying full attention to others while they speak, imagining yourself in their situation, and responding thoughtfully to their needs.

3. Finally, improving your communication skills is important for expressing yourself clearly and understanding others accurately. Focus on practicing your active listening skills, which involve fully concentrating on the speaker,

absorbing the message, and responding appropriately. **Effective communication** helps prevent misunderstandings and builds trust, making your interactions more productive and meaningful.

Chapter 5: Pathway to Personal Alignment and Fulfillment

Introduction

Do you feel your career aligns with your values and passions, bringing you joy, or do you feel unfulfilled and yearn for a deeper sense of purpose?

Embracing Change:
Overcoming Obstacles of Career Transitions

Recent trends show economic uncertainties and technological changes are pushing more professionals to consider career transitions. Many are seeking roles that offer better alignment with their personal values and career aspirations. Strategic planning, such as conducting a SWOT analysis, updating resumes, and enhancing online presence, is essential for successfully navigating these transitions (BusinessBecause).

Aligning your values, strengths, and passions will lead you toward achieving both personal and professional fulfillment. When your career and personal life truly reflect what matters most to you, the benefits go beyond simple job satisfaction. This alignment not only enhances your mental health and overall happiness but also makes you more productive, content, and able to make positive contributions to your environment.

In this chapter, we will explore why aligning these elements is so important and how it can transform your life and career into more satisfying and meaningful experiences. We'll discuss the profound impact that such alignment can have on your well-being and the quality of your contributions, both at work and in your personal life.

Understanding Personal Fulfillment

Understanding personal fulfillment involves exploring what makes you feel satisfied and content in both your personal life and career. It's about feeling that your daily activities resonate with your deepest values and contribute to your happiness.

Embracing Change:
Overcoming Obstacles of Career Transitions

The components of personal fulfillment include purpose, passion, and harmony between your personal and professional life. **Purpose** relates to having a clear understanding of your goals and feeling that your actions are meaningful. **Passion** involves engaging in activities that excite and motivate you, often those that align closely with your interests and talents. **Harmony** between your personal and professional life means managing both aspects so that one supports and enhances the other, rather than causing conflict or stress.

To assess your current levels of fulfillment in these areas, several tools and techniques can be useful. Self-assessment questionnaires can help you reflect on your current satisfaction levels and identify areas needing improvement. Regular journaling might also provide insights into your feelings about your life and career. Additionally, feedback from peers or mentors can offer an external perspective on how well your personal objectives align with your professional activities. By regularly evaluating these aspects of your life, you can make informed decisions that steer you toward greater fulfillment.

How can we balance building fulfilling

careers and nurturing the passions that

feed our souls?

Discovering Your Core Values

Discovering your core values is essential for leading a meaningful life, as these values influence your decisions in both personal and professional areas. When you are clear about what truly matters to you and can integrate these values into your daily life and work, you unlock a powerful pathway to purpose and happiness. Leveraging your strengths and pursuing passions that resonate with these values helps you to construct a fulfilling life vision.

Embracing Change:
Overcoming Obstacles of Career Transitions

To identify your personal values, try several reflective exercises. For instance, think about times you were happiest or felt very proud—these moments can highlight what you truly value. You can also consider qualities you admire in others, which often reflect your own values. Additionally, there are questionnaires and workshops designed to help you uncover your core values through structured exploration.

Your values play a significant role in shaping your life choices. They serve as a guiding compass, shaping your decisions, how you respond to different situations, and how well you fit within various environments or roles. For example, if creativity is a core value, you might prefer jobs that offer creative freedom and avoid those that feel restrictive or overly structured.

First, to ensure your daily activities and career choices reflect your values, evaluate how well your current lifestyle and job match your core values. If there's a discrepancy, consider what changes could bring them into closer alignment. This might involve changing jobs or adjusting how you approach your current role. Continuously checking and realigning your actions with your values is key to maintaining satisfaction and achieving long-term success. This proactive approach ensures that your actions and career path not only fulfill your immediate needs but also contribute to a deeper sense of purpose and satisfaction.

"The best way to predict the future is to create it." – Abraham Lincoln

---

Leveraging Your Strengths

Leveraging your strengths effectively can greatly enhance your career satisfaction and success. Start by recognizing what you're naturally good at. Tools like the **StrengthsFinder** assessment can help you identify these strengths by evaluating your responses to specific questions. Understanding your strengths allows you to make smarter choices about your career and personal growth.

Once you know your strengths, consider how to use them in your career. For example, if you excel at creativity and innovation, you might thrive in roles that involve design, marketing, or starting your own business. If you're already working, look for ways to adjust your job duties to better match your strengths, such as taking on projects that let you use these skills. This can lead to more job satisfaction and better opportunities for advancement.

It's also important to identify and develop strengths you haven't fully used yet. Exploring these can open new career opportunities and improve your performance. You might seek additional training, volunteer for new tasks at work, or start personal projects that let you practice these skills.

By focusing on these strategies—identifying, applying, and developing your strengths—you can build a career path that not only plays to your abilities but also challenges you to grow and achieve your potential.

Pursuing Your Passions

Pursuing your passions can be deeply fulfilling. Understanding what passion truly is and how it differs from mere hobbies or casual interests can help you make choices that lead to greater satisfaction.

Passion goes beyond hobbies, which are activities you might enjoy casually. Passion involves activities that you find deeply rewarding and feel a strong urge to engage in regularly. These are things that excite you, align with your core values, and make you feel energized.

To discover what you're passionate about, you need to explore and reflect. Try new things, revisit past interests, and pay attention to moments when you feel the most alive and engaged. Writing down when you feel most enthusiastic in a journal can help pinpoint your passions. Also, feedback from friends or family on when you seemed the most vibrant can help guide you.

Once you identify your passions, aim to align them with your career. This can make your work more enjoyable and fulfilling. Assess how your current job can incorporate your passions, perhaps by leading projects that match your interests or suggesting new ideas related to what you love. If your current role doesn't align well, consider looking for jobs or fields where your passions can be more central to your day-to-day tasks.

By clearly defining what passion means to you, actively seeking it out, and aligning it with your career, you can enhance your job satisfaction and overall happiness.

This approach makes your professional life more rewarding and enriches your personal life.

What would it feel like to live every day aligned with your deepest values and passions?

Practical Strategies for Alignment

Finding the right balance between your work and personal life leads to overall happiness and well-being. To achieve a balance that honors both your career goals and personal needs, it's important to set clear boundaries. Decide on specific times when work ends and personal time begins, ensuring you don't check work emails or take calls during your personal time. Also, make sure to carve out periods for activities that recharge you, like hobbies, exercise, or spending time with family and friends. Effective planning can help you manage both areas without one overshadowing the other.

Sometimes, you may find that your job doesn't align well with your personal values. If this happens, look for ways to reduce this conflict. You might explore different roles within your company that better match your values or discuss with your manager how your current role could be adjusted to fit your ethical views. If these adjustments aren't possible, it may be time to consider changing jobs to one that aligns more closely with your personal beliefs.

As your life and goals change, staying flexible and adjusting your balance is important. Regularly evaluate whether your current arrangement still works for your happiness and productivity. Be prepared to change your work commitments or personal activities to suit your evolving needs. This adaptability ensures that your professional and personal lives support each other in the best way possible.

By managing work-life integration, addressing conflicts between personal values and professional demands, and remaining adaptable, you can create a fulfilling balance that nurtures your personal satisfaction and professional success.

Chapter 6: Strategic Planning for Career Transition

Introduction

When planning your career change, do you

feel confident and strategic, or do you feel

unsure about your next steps?

Strategic planning is an essential tool for navigating successful career transitions. Just as a traveler needs to know their starting point to plan the best route, a professional must understand their strengths, weaknesses, opportunities, and threats (SWOT) to map out their career path effectively. This assessment helps to identify the skills and experiences that will distinguish you in the job market.

Embracing Change:
Overcoming Obstacles of Career Transitions

In this chapter, we'll help you assess your current skills, discuss the importance of performing a SWOT analysis to understand your position in the job market and identify areas that need improvement. You will learn how to research your target industry, pinpoint the necessary skills you need, and create a plan to develop those skills. We will also provide strategies for effective networking and financial planning to support your career transition, ensuring you have a comprehensive approach to achieving your professional goals.

Assessing Current Situation

Assessing your current career position through self-assessment and SWOT analysis can help you make informed decisions to improve job satisfaction and plan for future growth. First, closely examine your skills, interests, values, and where you currently stand in your career. Make a list of your skills, noting which areas are strong and which might need improvement. Reflect on what work activities keep you engaged and align these with your core values to see if your current job matches what's important to you. This process helps you understand your strengths and what you genuinely care about in your work.

After evaluating yourself, move on to performing a SWOT analysis. A SWOT analysis is a tool that helps you understand your current position in your career by examining four key areas: Strengths, Weaknesses, Opportunities, and Threats.

- **Strengths** are the areas where you excel. Think about what skills or experiences give you an edge over others in your field. Consider aspects like your professional network, specific technical skills, or soft skills like communication or leadership that make you stand out.

- **Weaknesses** are areas where you may lack certain skills or resources compared to others. Identifying these helps you understand where you need improvement. This might include gaps in your knowledge, limited experience in certain areas, or other personal limitations that could impact your career progress.

- **Opportunities** are external factors that you can take advantage of to advance your career. They might include trends in your industry that match your skills, new technologies that you can learn before they become mainstream, or networking events that can connect you with key people in your field.

- **Threats** are external challenges that could hinder your progress. They could be rising competition, changes in industry standards, or economic shifts that affect your job security or growth prospects.

By analyzing these four elements, you can create a clear strategy for your career development. You'll know where to focus your efforts to improve, what advantages you should leverage, and what external factors to prepare for, making your path forward clearer and more targeted.

Visualization and Clear Goal Setting

Positive visualization and effective goal setting are key techniques that can greatly improve your ability to reach your career goals. Visualization techniques, such as guided imagery and vision boards, help you clearly picture your career achievements. Guided imagery involves closing your eyes and vividly imagining yourself succeeding in your career goals, focusing on the actions you take and the feelings of success. Similarly, vision boards are collections of images and phrases that represent your goals. You display these boards where you can see them often to stay motivated and focused on what you want to achieve.

Setting effective goals using the SMART criteria can ensure your goals are clear and reachable. SMART stands for Specific, Measurable, Achievable, Relevant, and Time-bound. Specific goals clearly define what you want to achieve and answer the five Ws: Who, What, Where, When, and Why, Measurable goals allow you to track your progress, Achievable goals are realistic and attainable, Relevant goals align with your larger career objectives, and Time-bound goals have a deadline. By maintaining focus and structuring your goals around these parameters, you can create a clear roadmap for your career development that facilitates measurable steps. Regular review sessions to assess your progress and accountability partnerships to hold you responsible can greatly increase your motivation and commitment to achieving your goals.

Research and Information Gathering

Researching your target industry and keeping up with market trends are effective methods to prepare for future opportunities. Begin by thoroughly researching the industries, companies, and roles that interest you. Use online resources like company websites, industry blogs, and professional news outlets to gather detailed information. Another great way to gain insights is through informational interviews. Reach out to people who are working in the industry you're interested in; they can offer firsthand knowledge and advice that you won't find online. Joining professional groups and associations can also be beneficial. These organizations provide valuable networking opportunities, access to specialized resources, and sometimes exclusive industry data.

It's also important to stay informed about the latest trends and future projections in your field. Regularly read industry reports and professional publications to understand these trends. Attending conferences and seminars can give you insights from industry leaders and innovators, helping you see where your industry is headed. This knowledge helps you identify valuable skills to develop and positions you to take advantage of emerging opportunities.

By actively researching your industry and monitoring market trends, you'll be better equipped to make informed career decisions and adapt to changes, ensuring you're always prepared to seize new opportunities.

Skill Gap Analysis and Development Plan

Based on recent trends, as the job market evolves, there is a growing emphasis on continuous learning and skill development. Employers are prioritizing the upskilling and reskilling of their workforce to adapt to new technologies and job roles. This trend is crucial for employees looking to remain relevant and advance in their careers (Nexford University).

Embracing Change:
Overcoming Obstacles of Career Transitions

So, are you ready to turn your career goals into reality? It all begins with a clear grasp of your current position and the path you need to take. By developing and implementing a comprehensive strategy, you'll gain the necessary tools to successfully transition to your new career. Let's explore the steps you need to take to make this happen.

First, figure out which skills you need for your desired career path and how they compare to your current skills. Look at job listings in your target field to see the required skills and certifications. Then, compare these to your skills to see where you might need improvement.

Once you know your skill gaps, consider various ways to develop these skills. You can take online courses and certification training programs, attend workshops, or get practical experience through internships or volunteering. There are many resources available to help you learn new skills.

Next, put together a plan with clear steps and timelines to acquire the needed skills. Define what you want to achieve, list the activities you'll undertake (like specific courses or projects), and set deadlines for each. It's important to stay flexible and adjust your plan based on any new feedback or changes in your field.

To keep track of your progress, use tools like project management apps or simple checklists. These can help you manage deadlines and ensure you're meeting your goals. Regularly check your progress and adjust your plan if needed to stay on course.

By carefully identifying skill gaps, actively pursuing skill development, and closely monitoring your progress, you'll effectively prepare yourself for success in your new career direction. This strategy helps you close gaps in your skills and increases your confidence as you move forward.

Networking and Building Relationships

Networking and building strong professional relationships can open doors to new possibilities that you might not find through traditional job searches. These connections provide valuable insights, advice, and opportunities that can greatly influence your journey into a new field.

For effective networking, actively participate in industry-related events such as conferences, workshops, and local meetups. These gatherings are ideal for connecting with people who share your professional interests. During these events, engage in conversations and make sure to exchange contact information for future follow-ups.

Additionally, make the most of online platforms like LinkedIn. Update your profile to reflect your career goals, join groups relevant to your field, interact with posts, and connect with industry leaders. This can expand your network and increase your visibility within your chosen industry.

Another valuable strategy is to seek out mentors in your field. Mentors can provide personalized advice and guidance as you navigate your career transition. When approaching potential mentors, be clear about your goals, respectful of their time, and show a genuine interest in learning from their experiences. This approach offers valuable insights and support to help you achieve your career objectives.

Financial Considerations

Transitioning to a new career often brings unexpected expenses and changes in income that might catch you off guard. These can range from costs associated with additional training required for your new career path, costs for obtaining professional certifications, or expenses related to attending networking events and workshops. Moreover, you might encounter income disruptions if you lose your job due to industry changes or need to resign due to personal circumstances. Therefore, it's important to prepare a budget that accommodates these expenses. To prepare a budget, review your current expenses to identify potential savings and set aside funds specifically to cover the costs of education, certification programs, and other transition-related costs.

Additionally, managing financial risks both before and during the transition is equally important. Begin by setting up a savings plan that covers several months of living expenses. This financial cushion allows you to handle daily expenses comfortably, even if you experience a temporary loss of income. If possible, consider increasing your income with part-time work or freelance jobs, which can ease financial strain during this period. It's also wise to establish a contingency fund for unforeseen expenses, ensuring that unexpected financial needs do not disrupt your career transition plans.

Embracing Change:
Overcoming Obstacles of Career Transitions

Here are some key financial considerations to account for during a career transition:

1. **Income Fluctuations**: Transitioning to a new career can often lead to a period of reduced or no income, especially during a company downturn or if you decide to leave your job. It's important to plan for these gaps by saving sufficient funds to cover living expenses during this transition period.

2. **Cost of Education and Training**: Acquiring new skills or certifications may be necessary to enter a new field. This could mean enrolling in courses, attending workshops, or obtaining degrees, all of which can be costly. Budgeting for these expenses upfront can prevent financial stress later.

3. **Emergency Fund**: Building an emergency fund is more crucial than ever during a career transition. This fund can help you manage unexpected expenses and provide financial stability. Experts often recommend having at least three to six months' worth of living expenses saved in an easily accessible account.

4. **Long-term Financial Planning**: When considering a new career path, it's important to evaluate its long-term financial implications. Research the potential salary ranges, growth opportunities, and the stability of the industry. This information will help you determine if the career shift aligns with your long-term financial goals and ensure it's a sound investment in your future.

5. **Insurance and Benefits**: If changing careers results in the loss of employer-provided benefits, it's essential to secure health insurance and possibly other types of insurance on your own. Consider options such as COBRA, joining your spouse's insurance plan, or exploring a health insurance marketplace to maintain continuous coverage. Be sure to account for the costs of these benefits, which can be substantial, in your financial planning.

6. **Unemployment Benefits**: Check if you qualify for unemployment benefits and familiarize yourself with the application process. Keep in mind that not all voluntary resignations are eligible for benefits, but there may be exceptions depending on the specific circumstances of your case.

7. **Reduction in Lifestyle Expenses**: Review and adjust your budget to eliminate non-essential expenses. This could mean downsizing your living arrangements, cutting back on luxury spending, and reducing routine costs such as dining out and entertainment. Additionally, consider taking on part-time work, freelancing, or consulting in your field to keep some income coming in. These steps can alleviate financial pressure, allowing you to concentrate on your career transition.

8. **Investment in Professional Development**: In addition to formal education, investing in professional development through networking events, professional associations, and industry conferences is essential. While these

activities do require financial commitment, they can greatly enhance your visibility and appeal as a candidate in a new field.

By carefully planning and managing your finances, including saving for unexpected expenses and creating additional income streams, you can ensure a smoother and more financially secure career transition. This careful financial preparation allows you to focus on advancing your career without the stress of financial concerns.

Chapter 7: Executing Your Transition

Introduction

As you switch careers, do you feel ready to reshape your professional image and update your goals, or are you unsure where to start?

Embracing Change:
Overcoming Obstacles of Career Transitions

This chapter focuses on how to align your personal brand with your career goals effectively. Here, you'll discover the best ways to update your resume and enhance your online presence to highlight your key skills. We'll also provide essential tips for interview preparation, helping you respond to common questions and showcase your unique experiences. Additionally, you'll learn how to set a realistic timeline for your career change and establish achievable goals to keep you motivated throughout the process. These strategies are designed to guide you confidently and successfully through your career transition.

Developing a Personal Brand

Developing a strong personal brand reflects who you are professionally – it includes your expertise, values, and the unique qualities that you bring to the table. It helps you stand out in a competitive job market, especially during a career change.

The importance of a well-constructed personal brand cannot be overstated. In today's digital era, your online persona often makes the first impression. Think of your personal brand as your professional reputation. It's how people perceive your abilities and strengths in the workplace. During a career transition, establishing a strong personal brand can open doors to new opportunities and make you more attractive to potential employers in a new industry.

To develop your personal brand, start by identifying your unique value proposition (UVP). Your unique value proposition (UVP) is a clear concise statement that highlights what makes you distinct and valuable in your profession. To define your

UVP, consider your key strengths, past achievements, and what you're most passionate about in your work. This will help you articulate how you can contribute uniquely to a new role or industry.

Here's an example of a UVP for a professional in digital marketing:

> *"Empowering brands to amplify their voice: As a digital marketing specialist with over a decade of experience, I blend innovative content strategies with cutting-edge analytics to increase your online visibility and engagement. With a proven track record of increasing website traffic by up to 50% and tripling social media engagement for multiple clients, I help your brand not just compete, but dominate in a crowded digital landscape."*

This UVP highlights the individual's expertise, quantifiable achievements, and the specific benefits they bring to potential employers or clients, positioning them as a highly valuable candidate in their field.

Make sure your personal brand reflects your career goals. This involves updating your digital presence—like your LinkedIn profile, personal website, and professional bio—to showcase skills and experiences relevant to your new industry. For instance, modify your LinkedIn summary to emphasize qualities and expertise that align with your new career goals.

By understanding, articulating, and aligning your personal brand with your career goals, you create a powerful tool that supports your transition into a new industry.

This alignment helps you market yourself effectively and ensures you are seen as a valuable candidate perfectly suited for your new path.

Updating Your Resume and Online Presence

As you transition into a new career, it's essential to tailor your resume to highlight skills that are transferable to your new field, while minimizing less relevant experiences. Optimizing your LinkedIn profile and using other social media platforms can increase your visibility and help you network effectively.

When tailoring your resume for a career change, focus on highlighting skills that are valuable in your new field. Identify skills like leadership, communication, and problem-solving that are applicable across various industries, and make these prominent on your resume. Use keywords that are specific to the industry you're targeting and organize your resume, so the most relevant experiences are the most visible. For less relevant experiences, downplay them or frame them to emphasize any transferable skills.

Make sure your LinkedIn profile reflects your career change. Update your headline, summary, and the details of your past jobs to include industry-specific keywords and skills. Use LinkedIn or Facebook to engage with groups and discussions related to your new field to enhance your visibility and network. Use Instagram to showcase passion projects that align with your new career interests.

By carefully adjusting your resume and optimizing your online presence, you can effectively position yourself as a viable candidate within your new industry, increasing your chances of making a successful career transition.

Interview Preparation Techniques

Interviews can be intimidating, especially when you are venturing into a new professional arena. The key to success lies in preparation and understanding the perspective of potential employers. Preparing for interviews requires specific strategies to effectively communicate why you're a great fit for the role, despite any gaps in direct experience.

To prepare effectively for interviews, start by researching the company's mission, values, and culture to tailor your responses. Understand the role thoroughly by reviewing the job description and aligning your skills with the requirements. Engage in mock interviews with a trusted friend or mentor who can provide feedback and help refine your approach.

Practice answering common questions and use the STAR method (Situation, Task, Action, Result) to prepare stories highlighting your relevant skills. Have questions ready for the interviewer to demonstrate your interest.

A compelling way to connect with your interviewer is through storytelling. Prepare stories from your past experiences that align with the job you're applying for, focusing on how these experiences have prepared you for this new role. Also, consider what unique perspectives you bring to the table. Structure your stories to clearly illustrate the situation, the actions you took, and the outcomes. This method not only makes your answers more memorable but also demonstrates how your diverse experiences add value to your future aspirations and the potential employer.

Be prepared to address potential concerns an interviewer might have about your application, such as lack of direct experience in the field, being overqualified, or having gaps in your technical knowledge. For each concern, prepare a reasoned response that turns these perceived weaknesses into strengths or shows proactive steps you've taken to bridge the gaps. For example, if you lack specific technical skills, discuss how you are actively acquiring these skills through courses or projects. If there's concern about being overqualified, emphasize your commitment to the new path and how your extensive experience will bring a unique perspective and value to the team.

Could understanding the relationship between your story and practical preparation be the key to your next career breakthrough?

By thoroughly preparing for interviews, using storytelling to enhance your communication, and effectively addressing potential objections, you will present yourself as a well-rounded and adaptable candidate ready to transition into a new field confidently.

Transition Timelines and Setting Milestones

When changing careers, setting a realistic timeline and establishing clear milestones to guide your progress and keep you motivated is important. Start by defining your main goal, like getting a job in a new industry or starting a freelance business. Break down this goal into smaller, manageable steps. For instance, if your goal is to change industries, your initial steps might include researching a new field, updating your resume, and expanding your network. Assign realistic time frames to each step based on how much time you can dedicate each day or week. This timeline acts as your roadmap, helping you stay focused and on track.

Setting specific milestones is key to tracking your progress along with your timeline. Milestones are significant points along your timeline where you can evaluate your progress. For example, completing a certification course needed for your new career can be a milestone. Achieving these milestones provides a sense of accomplishment and keeps you motivated. Ensure your milestones are measurable and achievable, providing clear signs of your progress. Celebrating these milestones, no matter how small, can lift your spirits and motivate you to keep pushing forward.

By planning out a realistic timeline and setting achievable milestones, you create a structured approach to your career transition. This structured planning helps manage the complexity of changing careers and ensures you stay motivated and committed to reaching your new career goals.

Chapter 8: Overcoming Obstacles

Introduction

When changing careers, do you feel

prepared to face the challenges, or are you

unsure how to handle the obstacles ahead?

Understanding the hurdles you're likely to face and mastering effective strategies to overcome them is important for your personal and professional growth. We'll explore why these obstacles are often inevitable and how facing them can help you build the resilience needed to succeed. By recognizing and preparing for these obstacles, you'll be better equipped to overcome them and achieve significant progress in your journey.

Common Challenges in Career Transition

Navigating a career transition can be challenging due to several common obstacles. Understanding how to address these challenges can make your transition smoother and more successful.

One major challenge may be a **lack of industry-specific experience**. To compensate for this, emphasize transferable skills such as leadership, communication, and problem-solving that are valuable in any field. Additionally, consider obtaining certifications that are relevant to the new industry quickly. These can enhance your resume and demonstrate your commitment to entering the new field.

Older workers might face **ageism** in the job market. To counteract this, showcase your continual learning and adaptability. Highlight recent training or new skills you've acquired, and present your extensive experience as an asset, showing how it brings a valuable perspective and depth of knowledge to the workplace.

Sometimes, being seen as **overqualified** can prevent you from getting hired. Adjust your resume and interview responses to focus on how your extensive experience is a benefit, not a drawback. Frame your qualifications as enabling you to bring more to the role and to perform with a unique understanding and efficiency.

Fear of failure is a common emotional challenge. Practice mindfulness to stay calm and focused, and use cognitive restructuring to challenge negative thoughts, turning them into positive ones. Developing these coping mechanisms can help you navigate the uncertainties of changing careers with more confidence and less fear.

By addressing these challenges head-on with strategic approaches and a positive mindset, you can effectively manage the difficulties of career transitions and move towards a successful new phase in your professional life.

"It is never too late to be what you might have been." – George Eliot

---

Strategic Approaches to Overcome Barriers

When navigating career transitions, it's crucial to strategically overcome barriers that might hinder your move into a new field. One effective strategy is to focus on acquiring new skills that directly address gaps in your resume. Engage in targeted learning through online courses, workshops, or certifications relevant to the field you're entering. This enhances your skills and strengthens your candidacy, showing potential employers you are proactive and committed to your new career path.

It's important to update how you present yourself in the job market. Adjust your resume and LinkedIn profile to align your past experiences with your new career goals. Highlight transferable skills and frame your previous work experience in a way that appears beneficial for the roles you are targeting. This rebranding helps potential employers see how your background is relevant and an asset to the new field.

Employ creative problem-solving techniques to stand out. Conduct informational interviews with people already working in your target industry to gain insights and advice. Consider shadowing professionals to understand the day-to-day demands of the job or engaging in volunteer work related to the field. These activities give you real insights, build your credibility, and can open doors to new opportunities.

The ability to adapt to changing circumstances and expectations is important in today's job market. Highlight your flexibility in your applications and interviews, emphasizing your ability to learn and succeed in different environments. Employers value candidates who can handle the evolving demands of the industry and are prepared to tackle new challenges.

By focusing on these strategic approaches—developing relevant skills, rebranding yourself, using creative problem-solving, and demonstrating adaptability—you can effectively overcome the barriers to a successful career transition and position yourself as a strong candidate in your new field.

Leveraging Support Systems

No journey is meant to be traveled alone, and this is particularly true when transitioning careers. **Leveraging your support system** is not just about seeking guidance; it's about enriching your journey with different perspectives and emotional encouragement. When changing careers, having a strong support system can be invaluable. It's important to join professional associations and networks related to your new industry. These groups provide access to resources, learning opportunities, and networking events that can connect you with potential employers and experienced professionals. They provide a platform where you can seek advice and learn from others who have a deep understanding of the industry.

Finding a mentor or a career coach can greatly enhance your transition experience. A mentor, usually an experienced professional in your field, can offer you guidance, support, and an insider's perspective on how to succeed. They can also help you navigate industry norms and introduce you to their professional contacts. Similarly, a career coach can help you clarify your career goals, refine your resume, and sharpen your interview skills.

Joining community groups or online forums for people experiencing career changes can also be beneficial. These groups provide emotional support and practical advice from others who are experiencing similar challenges. They can offer job tips, encouragement, and sometimes even job leads. Engaging in discussions and sharing experiences with peers who are also changing careers can help you feel supported and less isolated during your transition.

By actively participating in professional networks, seeking mentorship, and engaging with community and peer groups, you can surround yourself with a supportive network, gain valuable insights, build confidence, and find encouragement as you navigate your career journey.

How strong is your support system to help you

stay stable during uncertain times in your

career?

Tools & Resources

Changing careers is a significant step that requires careful planning, resilience, and ongoing learning. To aid in your career transition, a variety of resources are available to support your progress:

1. **Courses and Additional Support:**

    a. *The Training Lounge, LLC*, (www.TheTrainingLounge.com) specializes in services designed to increase personal and professional growth. They offer training and development, support for career transitions, professional development programs, educational online courses, and group coaching. These services are tailored to help individuals enhance their skills and achieve their career objectives.

b. *LinkedIn Learning*, (www.LinkedIn.com) provides courses to help you gain new skills and knowledge.

2. **Self-Assessment Tools and Development Action Plans:**

a. *Myers-Briggs Type Indicator (MBTI)*, (www.themyersbriggs.com), is a psychological test that helps people understand how they perceive the world and make decisions. The results offer insights into your natural strengths and how you interact with others, which can be useful for personal growth, career planning, and improving relationships.

b. *StrengthsFinder assessment*, (www.gallup.com/cliftonstrengths) now known as CliftonStrengths, is a developmental tool designed to help individuals identify, understand, and maximize their strengths. Individuals can use the insights from the assessment to guide their career development, improve their performance in current roles, or explore new roles where their strengths can be more fully utilized.

c. *SMART* goals are a widely used framework for setting clear, achievable objectives. The acronym SMART stands for Specific, Measurable, Achievable, Relevant, and Time-bound. The SMART goal framework helps ensure that objectives are well-thought-out, structured, and trackable, increasing the likelihood of achieving them. This method can be used for personal development, project management, or business planning.

3. **Recommended Books:**

a. *Transforming Within: Addressing Emotional and Psychological Aspects of Career Change by Treva Bendy* - This book provides a comprehensive roadmap for navigating the intricate emotional and psychological landscape of career transformation, equipping you with the strategies and insights needed to make a confident and successful transition.

b. *Mindset Shift: Transitioning to a Career in Instructional Design by Treva Bendy* - This book is your guide and mentor on the journey to a career in instructional design, focusing on the mental and emotional aspects of this career transition. Packed with reflective prompts, inspiring quotes, and practical advice, it's designed to nurture your transition into the dynamic field of instructional design.

c. *Transitions: Making Sense of Life's Changes by William Bridges* - This book provides a thorough look at the process of transitions in personal and professional life, offering guidance on how to deal with changes constructively.

d. *Pivot: The Only Move That Matters Is Your Next One by Jenny Blake* - This guide is great for anyone looking to make a calculated move within their current career path or into a new field. It focuses on finding new opportunities and expanding your career without starting from scratch.

e. *Designing Your Life: How to Build a Well-Lived, Joyful Life by Bill Burnett and Dave Evans* - Based on a popular Stanford University course, this book uses design thinking to approach career changes, helping readers build a career that is fulfilling and aligned with their interests and strengths.

f. *The First 90 Days: Proven Strategies for Getting Up to Speed Faster and Smarter* by Michael D. Watkins - Ideal for those transitioning into new roles, this book offers strategies to help you excel during the crucial first three months of a new position.

g. *Reinventing You: Define Your Brand, Imagine Your Future* by Dorie Clark - This book is a step-by-step guide to assessing your unique strengths and defining your personal brand, helping you make a name for yourself in a new industry or role.

h. *Working Identity: Unconventional Strategies for Reinventing Your Career* by Herminia Ibarra - This book provides a fresh perspective on career change, emphasizing the importance of experimentation and the iterative process in finding the right career path.

i. *What Color Is Your Parachute?* by Richard N. Bolles - A comprehensive job-hunting guide updated annually to reflect current job market conditions and new job-seeking strategies. The book is well-known for its practical and effective approach to career planning and has been a popular resource for job seekers for decades.

j. *Switchers: How Smart Professionals Change Careers and Seize Success* by Dawn Graham - The book addresses the unique challenges faced by career switchers, including overcoming the bias against candidates without "direct" experience, and how to rebrand oneself to fit into a new industry or job.

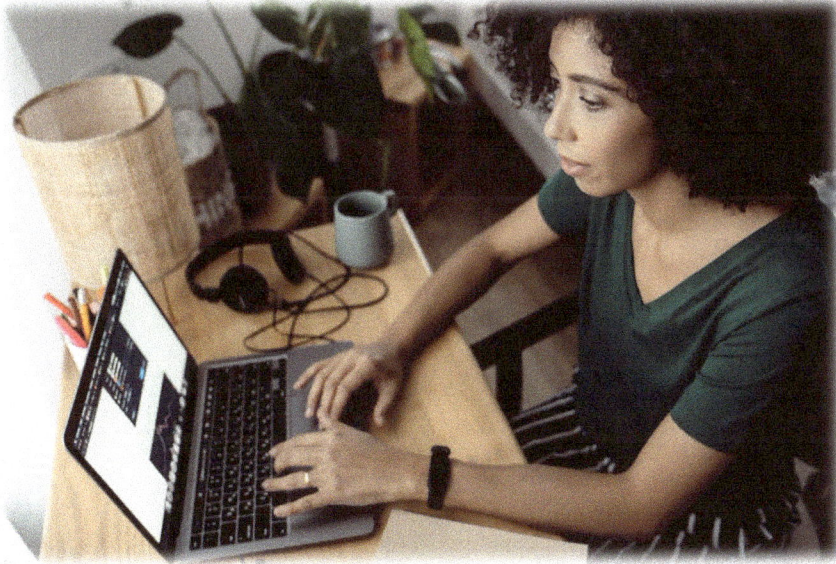

Could exploring these resources be the key to unlocking the door to your new career?

Conclusion

Remember, the path to a fulfilling career is not linear. It requires patience, persistence, and most importantly, a willingness to embrace change. As you move forward, keep revisiting the lessons learned and continuously seek out new knowledge and experiences. With the strategies and insights provided, you are well-equipped to embark on your next career adventure, ensuring it is both successful and rewarding.

Embracing Change:
Overcoming Obstacles of Career Transitions

"The only way to do great work is to love what you do." – Steve Jobs

---

Ready to Take the Next Step?

Navigating a career transition can be challenging, but you don't have to do it alone. Whether you're looking to advance in your current field or pivot to a new one, The Training Lounge provides the tools and guidance necessary for success. At **The Training Lounge**, our comprehensive online platform offers:

- Training and development programs
- Career transition support
- Professional development courses
- Educational online courses
- Group coaching sessions

Each service is designed to help you enhance your skills and achieve your career goals. Visit **The Training Lounge** at www.TheTrainingLounge.com to **explore our services** and **schedule a Career Strategy Call**. Let us help you navigate your career path with confidence!

Wrap Up

By maintaining an open mind and a proactive attitude, you can transform potential obstacles into steppingstones for growth and achievement. Your career transition is not just a job change; it's an important chapter in your life's story, full of opportunities for personal development and professional satisfaction. Embrace this journey with optimism and courage and remember that each step forward brings you closer to realizing your true potential and achieving your career aspirations. Best wishes, and here's to all the great things you will achieve!

Take Action Now!

Take Action Now! is designed to help you reflect on and align with your career and personal goals. This section compiles the thought-provoking questions from throughout the book, providing space for you to think through and write your answers as you encounter each question. It's structured to help you think deeply and act purposefully on your journey.

Chapter 1: Understanding Career Transitions

1. When you wake up for work in the morning, do you feel invigorated and ready to take on new challenges, or do you find yourself counting the minutes until the day ends?

2. How could understanding the specific type of career transition you are undergoing change how you prepare for your future?

Chapter 2: The Catalysts of Change

3. As jobs change with technology and the economy, are you excited to explore new career opportunities, or do you feel pressured to rethink your current path?

4. Are you listening to subtle cues from your professional life, or are you ignoring them?

_____

_____

_____

_____

_____

_____

_____

_____

_____

Chapter 3: The Emotional and Psychological Journey

5. When considering a career change, do you feel excited about new opportunities, or do you find yourself uncertain about leaving your familiar work environment?

_____

_____

_____

_____

_____

_____

_____

_____

6. Could recognizing and embracing each phase of this emotional rollercoaster be the key to mastering your career transition?

_____

_____

_____

_____

_____

_____

_____

_____

Chapter 4: Cultivating the Right Mindset for Career Transition

7. During your career change, do you face each day with a positive mindset, eager to embrace new challenges, or do you struggle to adapt and overcome obstacles?

_____

_____

_____

_____

_____

_____

_____

_____

8. Could recognizing and fostering a growth mindset be the key to unlocking your full potential in your career transition?

9. Was there a specific moment when you realized how important adaptation is in your career?

Chapter 5: Pathway to Personal Alignment and Fulfillment

10. Do you feel your career aligns with your values and passions, bringing you joy, or do you feel unfulfilled and yearn for a deeper sense of purpose?

11. How can we balance building fulfilling careers and nurturing the passions that feed our souls?

12. What would it feel like to live every day aligned with your deepest values and passions?

_____

_____

_____

_____

_____

_____

_____

_____

Chapter 6: Strategic Planning for Career Transition

13. When planning your career change, do you feel confident and strategic, or do you feel unsure about your next steps?

_____

_____

_____

_____

_____

_____

_____

Chapter 7: Executing Your Transition

14. As you switch careers, do you feel ready to reshape your professional image and update your goals, or are you unsure where to start?

_____

_____

_____

_____

_____

_____

_____

_____

15. Could understanding the relationship between your story and practical preparation be the key to your next career breakthrough?

_____

_____

_____

_____

_____

_____

_____

_____

Chapter 8: Overcoming Obstacles

16. When changing careers, do you feel prepared to face the challenges, or are you unsure of how to handle the obstacles ahead?

_____

_____

_____

_____

_____

_____

_____

_____

_____

17. How strong is your support system to help you stay stable during uncertain times in your career?

_____

_____

_____

_____

_____

_____

_____

_____

_____

18. Could exploring these resources be the key to unlocking the door to your new career?

www.ingramcontent.com/pod-product-compliance
Lightning Source LLC
Chambersburg PA
CBHW050038220326
41599CB00040B/7197